to Aaron Copland

SONATINA

George A...
(1932)
edited by Ron Erickson

* m.12: All ♮s in mm. 12-15 are editorial.

** m.12, ms.: F, not E.

8

* m.141: time values are in the ms., but this measure needs either a change of meter or of time value.

** m.142, ms.: a middle staff is included here for the violin. The pizz. indication for the cello may include the violin, which would present a technical difficulty to be resolved by the players.

* m.121: ms.: this tie comes just before a page break and is not continued on the following page.
** m.127, ms.: G.A.'s original arco was changed to pizz., in ink, by an unknown hand.
    Pizz./arcos following, in parentheses, are also not in G.A.'s hand but are also in ink.

SONATINA

to Aaron Copland

George Antheil
(1932)
edited by Ron Erickson

* m.12: All ♮s in mm. 12-15 are editorial.

** m.12, ms.: F, not E.

* m.141: time values are in the ms., but this measure needs either a change of meter or of time value.

** m.142, ms.: a middle staff is included here for the violin. The pizz. indication for the cello may include the violin, which would present a technical difficulty to be resolved by the players.

* m.121: ms.: this tie comes just before a page break and is not continued on the following page.
** m.127, ms.: G.A.'s original arco was changed to pizz., in ink, by an unknown hand.
  Pizz./arcos following, in parentheses, are also not in G.A.'s hand but are also in ink.

* m.70, ms.: C♮, B♭, B♮, A♮.

* m.70, ms.: C♮, B♭, B♮, A♮.

102

105

107

[*ff* brillante]

[*ff* brillante]

109

112

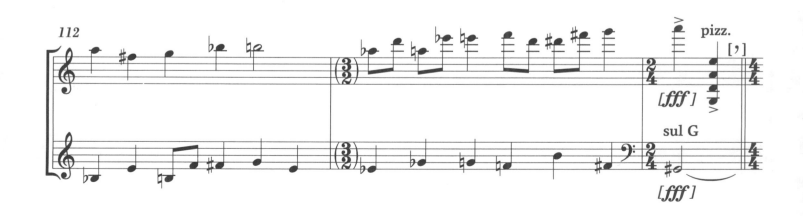